WILD HARVESTERS

Wild Harvesters

The first people in Scotland

Bill Finlayson

Series editor: Gordon Barclay

CANONGATE BOOKS
with
HISTORIC  SCOTLAND

THE MAKING
OF SCOTLAND

Series editor:
Gordon Barclay

Other titles available:

FARMERS, TEMPLES AND TOMBS:
Scotland in the Neolithic
and Early Bronze Age

SETTLEMENT AND SACRIFICE:
The Later Prehistoric People
of Scotland

A GATHERING OF EAGLES:
Scenes from Roman Scotland

First published in Great Britain in 1998
by Canongate Books Ltd, 14 High
Street, Edinburgh EH1 1TE

British Library Cataloguing-in-Publication Data
A catalogue record for this book is available on request
from the British Library

ISBN 0 86241 779 1

Series Design:
James Hutcheson, Canongate Books

Design:
Stephen Chester

Printed and bound by
GraphyCems

Previous page
The rocky west coast of
Scotland, an area inhabited
by Scotland's first settlers.

Contents

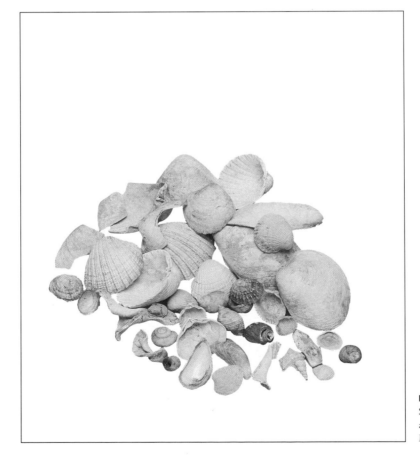

Mesolithic Midden
Shell remains found in a midden dating to the Mesolithic period.

After the Ice Age

This book is an introduction to the first people to live in Scotland. Relatively little is known about them – indeed it is only in the last 50 years or so that we have discovered their existence. They left none of the great monuments that later cultures built, the tombs, stone circles, hill forts and so on that are recognised as archaeological sites and can still be visited today. The period they lived in is covered by this book and is called the Mesolithic.

People first moved into the country after the end of the last Ice Age, about 10,000 years ago. They lived before the development of farming and had to get their food from the wild – fish, nuts, berries, and wild animals both large and small. They had no villages or even proper houses and had to be fairly mobile to take advantage of the different resources they needed, moving from place to place at different times of year. This way of life is known as hunter-gathering: hunting wild animals and gathering plant foods. Today this way of life only survives in a few, generally marginal, environments, such as the Australian outback and the Kalahari desert. Even in these places there are few, if any, who still survive entirely on natural resources. This makes it particularly difficult for us to study or imagine how the first people in Scotland lived, as their way of life was so different from ours. Also, as they built no houses, no temples and no forts, there seems at first little left from their life with which to study them today.

Scottish Pine Forest *(opposite)*
Ten thousand years of human occupation and changing land use have left few areas that resemble what the first people to arrive will have seen.
CAROLINE WICKHAM-JONES

Hunter-gatherers
Contemporary hunter-gatherers in southern Africa give us some understanding of how Mesolithic societies may have lived.
ALAN BARNARD

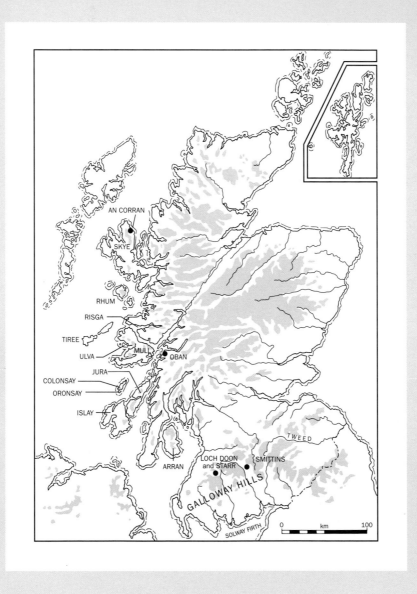

AN CORRAN

SKYE

RHUM

RISGA

TIREE

ULVA

MULL

OBAN

JURA

COLONSAY

ORONSAY

ISLAY

TWEED

ARRAN

LOCH DOON
and STARR

SMITTINS

GALLOWAY HILLS

SOLWAY FIRTH

0   km   100

Because of these difficulties we have to use a wide range of methods to learn about them. Of course we use the techniques of archaeology: the excavation of the camp sites these people lived in and the study of their stone, bone and antler tools, but we also have to use the techniques of botany and zoology to study the materials left in their rubbish heaps or middens to understand what they ate, how big or old it was when they caught it, and during which season they lived at each site. Furthermore, we have to use anthropology – the study of modern peoples – to gain some insight into the hunter-gatherer mind and way of life. In addition, we must interpret our results in the light of what other archaeologists have found out in other parts of Europe, because, while Scotland is particularly rich in some types of evidence, especially shell waste middens, it is poor in others, such as burials. The study of hunter-gatherers depends very much on combining these different strands of evidence.

Part of the fascination of studying these early people is in the search to understand them, in the development of the methods and theories which allow us to approach them. Another challenge results from how very different their lives were from ours. It is difficult to understand the way people survived, had families, and what they thought of the world, at such a distance from our own times. However, these people are our ancestors – the first to live in Scotland. A little bit of them will have come down to shape the way Scotland and indeed the Scots have developed. There have been changes since then and many new people have arrived, but from these earliest colonists onwards, through their interaction with the environment, the people living in Scotland have developed their own distinctive way of doing things.

In this book, I will try to show what we know of these hunter-gatherers and how we know it. I will explain how these people, despite living from 10,000 to 6000 years ago, with no farms and no houses, were in many ways like us. Physically they were modern humans, the same as we are. Their brains were the same as ours. We can never hope to know how they spoke, but we do know that they will have spoken a language rich in the words they needed to describe their environment. Indeed, through their way of life, they will have had a hugely rich understanding of this environment. People are superb at adapting to their conditions and while our modern conditions require that we know how to survive in cities, how to drive cars, use computers and so on, their's required that they knew how to survive in the natural environment, and they succeeded for thousands of years. They were not primitive savages grubbing out an existence close to the subsistence margin, but had a very

Location Map *(opposite)*
Map showing principal areas mentioned in text.

Kalahari San
Women digging up tubers. Plant foods
have always been important to hunter-
gatherers. In most societies we know
the bulk of plant foods are collected
by women.
ALAN BARNARD

successful economy. Also,
as modern people, living
together and meeting other
groups, having families,
arguing, grieving, rejoicing
and doing all the things that
make up a human society,
they will have had a rich
culture. However, much of
the material evidence for this,
the symbols that showed what
group they belonged to, how
important they were and so
on, would have been made
of perishable materials and
so have been lost to us.

Because of the mobile
lifestyle employed by most
hunter-gatherers, I will not
describe the archaeological
sites as isolated entities, but
rather will describe a
patchwork made up of a
number of sites, showing
how people used the different
parts of their environment to
provide different resources. I will look at how they did not just
wander the landscape collecting and hunting, but at how they
would have had carefully established strategies, how they would
have used their knowledge of the weather to predict when it was
time to move, how they would have sent out task teams to
specific areas, and, perhaps most significantly, how they would
have modified their environment. I will use evidence from
pollen studies to show the establishment of clearings in woods,
along with evidence from Colonsay for huge hazelnut harvests
that probably required large gatherings of people, and how to
encourage such a harvest they may have had to burn clearings,
and prune the trees. I will examine how such an investment in
a resource implies a concept of ownership, not necessarily the
same as ours, but a resource identified with a people, even if
they did not live beside the resource all the time, but only came
to it when it was ripe. As a way of giving life to these different
theories, one of the techniques used in this book is to use an
imaginative reconstruction, following a group of hunter-
gatherers as they make use of different resources at different sites
through the year.

Stone Age Stereotypes

'Man the hunter' is a dominant image from pre-farming societies, with wild hairy men chasing big dangerous animals. While we should not deny that hunting would have been an important activity, we must understand its place in the overall economy and society. Hunting for large animals is often a relatively high risk means of getting food compared to more predictable resources such as fish, shellfish, nuts and fruit. It can, however, be an important part of the diet as well as providing additional non-food materials, such as skins, furs, sinew and bones for tool manufacture.

Today we tend to think of hunting as either involving large groups of people, perhaps most typically in Scotland in grouse shooting, or as a solo activity, where a man stalks and hunts alone, or with a small group of friends, equipped with a

North-eastern Asian Hunters
There are very few hunter-gatherer societies today so old records provide a useful source of information.
COURTESY OF CAROLINE WICKHAM-JONES

powerful rifle for deer or the latest in high-tech fishing tackle for salmon. All these types of hunting have a social element to them, and bringing home food is only part of the activity. Our association with men as the hunters comes as much from this modern view of hunting as it does from our knowledge of hunter-gatherer societies or the past. Hunting amongst hunter-gatherers is a rather different activity. Hunting does not just provide food. It is also not so much about the thrill of the chase, or the moment of the kill, although these will inevitably have played their part and success in hunting may have been important to a man's status. Hunting is about catching a resource as economically as possible, whether that is done by traps, nets, fishing lines, spears or bows and arrows. It is also about butchering a carcass and taking the useful parts away for processing. Big animals may well have more meat on them than is wanted, and consequently much of the meat has to be processed, by drying or smoking soon after the kill, before it goes bad, perhaps even before the journey home. Often, while big animal hunting may be done by the men in a group, much hunting of smaller prey is done by the women, as is much of the processing of the carcass. It is also important to remember the importance of fishing, especially in a country like Scotland, where both coastal waters and rivers will have been rich with fish (in fact, the more accurate term for the people we are studying should be hunter-gatherer-fishers).

Much of our modern understanding of hunter-gatherers comes from studies of modern or recent hunter-gatherers, people like the San in southern Africa, most of whom live in or around the Kalahari desert, the Eskimos and other northern peoples, who live around the Arctic, or aboriginals from Australia. However, there are a few very serious problems with using these as analogies for the Mesolithic in Scotland. The first is that they are modern societies, and just because they live a hunter-gatherer lifestyle, we should not forget that 6-10,000 years separates them from our hunter-gatherers. The second is that all modern studies of these peoples see them as they are now, living in contact with the modern world, not as they were before contact. Indeed, many modern hunter-gatherers have at times lived at least partially by farming, or have had a close relationship with farmers with whom they trade. The third, and perhaps the most significant divergence, is that modern hunter-gatherers tend to live in marginal environments such as deserts or arctic wastes, where farming is impossible. Our hunter-gatherers lived in a rich temperate environment, full of resources, so full indeed that we can suggest a number of different economic strategies they could have adopted. Therefore, although the information we can gain

from hunter-gatherer anthropology may be useful, we have to be careful how we use it. More than that, if we are interested in the past, we have to examine the past to see how human society has developed and changed. We must not just take modern examples and put them back into history.

Like us, as people, early hunter-gatherers will have had complicated social relationships within and between families. Their emotions and fears would be familiar to us. Their lifestyle will, however, have been sufficiently different from ours for them to have developed other ways of resolving their conflicts. The ways modern people have imagined Stone-Age societies have often been something of a caricature of our own times and prejudices. Hunter-gatherers have been seen as noble savages (as, for example, in 18th century images of American Indians), as

Modern Hunter-gatherer
When modern hunter-gatherers are used as a source of information it is important to remember that they are modern, not preserved prehistoric relics. All modern hunter-gatherers trade with settled communities and it is not unusual to see apparently odd combinations of traditional crafts and Western goods.
ALAN BARNARD

American Indians in the 17th century
Our impressions of other cultures are always coloured by our own background.
This French artist's representation from the 17th century is clearly a product of the
artist's culture, and reflects then current ideas concerning the 'noble savage'.

hairy cavemen beating each other on the head with clubs, and in the 1960s as peace-loving individuals who resolved all conflicts by debate or by simply agreeing to split up and go their separate ways. All of these models are the result of our looking back at so-called primitives from our point of view as civilised people. Even the idealistic 1960s view depends upon a belief that without ownership of houses, pots and so on and without the investment of labour in fields and stored foods, conflicts could be easily resolved. I hope to be able to make it clear that these people were not so very different from us – they didn't live in a Stone-Age never-never land, but would have had ideas of territory and of resources and objects belonging to people. Having said that, we should not underestimate just how different their view of the world may have been.

As archaeologists, we build up our own images of life in the past. We may claim greater sophistication, but when we want to provide a quick picture, we often fall back on the shorthand of our own stereotypes. Compare the picture below of hunter-gatherers with the picture overleaf of early farmers both found in a recent book. The first picture shows the Mesolithic, and is an image of rather desperate Robinson Crusoe-type characters, all men,

Hunter-gatherer Landscape
A reconstruction of a Mesolithic landscape.
ALAN BRABY, HISTORIC SCOTLAND

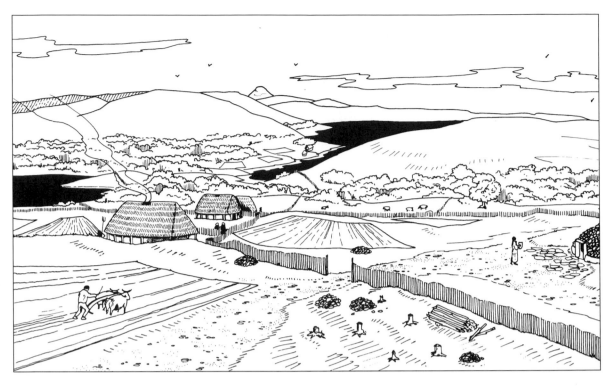

Early Farming Landscape

A reconstruction of a Neolithic
landscape, cleared and domesticated.
ALAN BRABY, HISTORIC SCOTLAND

wearing roughly stitched skins and hunting in a wild wood. The
second picture (above) is of farmers from the Neolithic; the
landscape has become tamed and, as if to emphasise this, we can
see a woman holding a baby. The author of that book does not
consider hunter-gatherers as early farmers in this rather
stereotypical way, and indeed this book reflects the very different
aspects of Mesolithic life, but these pictures do show just how
difficult it is for us to escape such powerful, inherited images.
The shaggy Robinson Crusoe image is of someone who has
been isolated from his culture, and who cannot cope; whereas
the hunter-gatherers of Scotland were in fact living within a
flourishing, functioning society.

Archaeologists call the period after the last Ice Age before
farming began the Mesolithic, which simply means the Middle
Stone Age, but this is just because apart from stone tools used by
the hunter-gatherers, few other objects survive on most sites.
The acid soils of Scotland have destroyed most other tools and
artefacts, but we know from shell midden sites in Scotland, and
from occasional sites scattered across Europe, that Mesolithic
people made bone and antler tools, they made baskets and fish
traps, they lined their floors with bark, and that they built canoes
and decorated elegant paddles.

So, what we need to do is to forget the convenient labels of
Stone Age, or cave men, and to consider the evidence we have
for this period.

Island Hopping

The canoe moved into the bay. The boy sitting at the prow could see that already a large number of other boats were drawn up on the beach, and that camp fires had been lit. He looked back to his sister, who had finally fallen asleep. This would be the first time she had seen so many people in one place. He hoped that this year he would be allowed to go off with the men to fish, while the women collected shells for bait, smoked the fish to store for later in the year and spent the days making the fine leather clothes that his people wore. They would mostly eat shellfish for the next few weeks and he was looking forward to this, even if his brother told him he would be sick of the sight of them before they left the island.

On the island of Oronsay a number of shell middens have been found, piles of shells discarded in great heaps around the old shoreline of the island. These were first examined by antiquarians in the last century, but are best understood through the work of archaeologist Paul Mellars who excavated there in the 1970s. Several very important studies have been made of the material he collected. The collections are particularly well preserved, as the calcium from the shells in the mound produces a less acidic microenvironment than most Scottish soils. Apart from the shells themselves, the type of material recovered includes mammal bones, bone and antler tools, flints and fish and bird bones. Much of the evidence Mellars recovered had not been found in the 19th century as it required careful sieving to pick out the fragments of fish bone. He was soon able to show that although the shells formed the bulk of the mounds, the presence of quantities of fish bones suggests that fish may have been more important to the diet than shellfish. Anyone who has eaten a plate of mussels will know that the size of the mound of shells is far greater than the amount eaten. Another suggestion put forward was that the limpets which form an important part of the mounds were not

Oronsay Middens
Shell middens are not always immediately recognisable as they are now mostly covered by grass.
IAN RALSTON

At Work and Play

The illustration shows people at work and
play on a beach camp site. People are busy cooking,
smoking fish to store for later, preparing shellfish,
making and repairing tools, nets and clothes.
Harpoons are standing outside their shelters. In the
distance you can see the smoke rising from a campsite on another
island. The people are dressed in well-made clothes and wear shells and tooth
beads. We do not know exactly how they were dressed – or how they wore the
beads we find – but we believe that like more recent hunter-gatherers, they will
have cared for their personal appearance.

HARRY BLAND

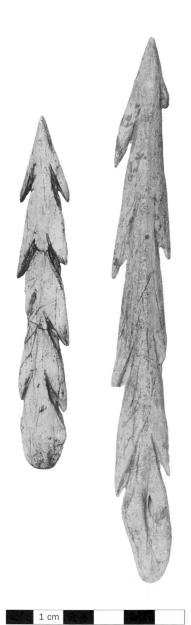

Bone and Antler Tools

These harpoons are typical examples of
the fine workmanship recovered from
shell middens on the west coast.
NATIONAL MUSEUMS OF SCOTLAND

collected for eating, but as bait for fishing. Limpets are a very
rubbery shellfish to eat and would certainly appear to be a
peculiar choice for people who also had fish and oysters to eat.

One of the best pieces of detective work on the material
from the Oronsay middens was conducted on the tiny bones
called otoliths which come from a fish called the saithe. One
student studying these fish bones observed that the sizes of the
saithe otoliths differed from midden to midden. He began a
programme of experimental studies and was able to show that
the different sizes could be linked very closely to the age of the
fish. Looking at the behaviour of modern saithe he was able to
show that the size of fish depended upon the time of year. From
this he was able to show that the different sizes of otoliths found
at the various Mesolithic middens meant that people were
coming to these middens at different times of year, and that in
general the middens were each occupied for particular seasons.
Exactly why they were doing this is more difficult to establish,
but it seems to represent a pattern that continued for a
considerable number of years. Some scholars have suggested that
the same group of hunter-gatherers lived on Oronsay all year,
and moved on periodically around the island in a steady and
constant progression, perhaps because of the weather, or perhaps
as they used up the closest shellfish.

However, I do not believe that this is the most likely course
of events. During the time when the middens were
accumulating, Oronsay was an even smaller island than it is now,
as the sea level was higher than at present, so the population
would have been restricting itself to a very small world at a time
when we know that groups were much more mobile than
people now. Oronsay would have had few, if any, of the other
resources, plant or animal, needed for survival. Indeed, the
mammal bones from the middens suggest that people had
contacts outwith the island – the size of the bones suggests that at
least two different populations of deer were being hunted: one of
rather small deer, probably from a population that had become
isolated on an island for a very long time, and the other of larger
deer, from a bigger population. It seems unlikely that the small
deer would have come from the neighbouring island of
Colonsay, as that island is probably too far from anywhere else
for deer to have become established, which would suggest that
they must be from an island closer to the mainland, perhaps Jura.
The larger deer were probably hunted on the mainland. This
suggests a pattern of wider ranging contacts.

In addition, the particular fragments of bone that have been
recovered are not typical of those you would transport in your
boat if you were interested in meat. The collection has a

Shell Midden Material
This is a collection of the sort of refuse that is
contained in shell middens.
NATIONAL MUSEUMS OF SCOTLAND

1 cm

Antler Mattock
Antler mattocks may have had a range of functions,
perhaps including digging for tubers.
NATIONAL MUSEUMS OF SCOTLAND

Excavation Methods
Mesolithic sites are mostly short term camp sites and the evidence can be
very slight. At the excavations on Rhum fine sieving was conducted to
recover small artefacts, bones, seeds and other small remains.
CAROLINE WICKHAM-JONES

surprisingly large proportion of non-meat bearing bones. This at first appears confusing: why carry parts of animal skeletons all the way to Oronsay if they were no good for eating? The answer to this may explain why people were going back to the same places on Oronsay again and again. There was no need to take meat foods to Oronsay because there were enough fish and shellfish to keep your group fed. What is more, if you knew where the saithe were going to be, and you could predict the shellfish quantities, you would have a very secure and predictable resource. For a few weeks it would be possible for at least part of the group to stay in one place, which would allow them to get on with the various chores that had to be done. One of these was the manufacture of the bone and antler tools that were needed and it is the case that the bone parts taken to Oronsay are the same as those used to make tools, so we can suggest that while part of the group went fishing, another part stayed by the middens making bone tools, such as harpoons.

They also made another tool, a bevel-ended tool shape which has caused some arguments between archaeologists since it was first identified (see p.25). It has been suggested that this tool was used for knocking limpets off rocks, or scooping out the

Saithe
Preserved within the shell middens on Oronsay were the bones of fish. One of the most important was the saithe.
BILL FINLAYSON

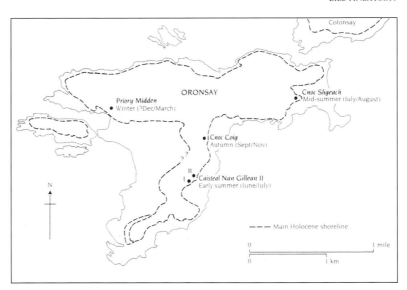

Oronsay Shorelines
Shorelines have changed since the Mesolithic. This plan shows how much smaller Oronsay was when the people who left the middens lived there.
OXFORD UNIVERSITY PRESS

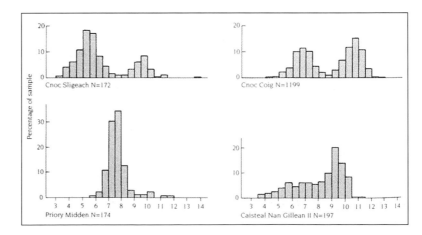

Otolith Size Graphs
Studying the size distribution of saithe otolith sizes and comparing these with modern samples allows us to determine at which seasons the different middens were used.
OXFORD UNIVERSITY PRESS

limpet from within its shell. The presence of these tools in the shell middens has been used to support this argument. This is an example of how modern people tend to assume that life in the Mesolithic was a fairly grim struggle for survival, and that all tools would have been directly related to the business of collecting food. I would argue that these tools are leather working tools and that as well as making tools at the midden sites, people were also using the tools to make leather clothing. This theory may help us to explain why different

Modern Hide Dressing Experiments
Experimenting with prehistoric tasks gives insight into how tools functioned.
CAROLINE WICKHAM-JONES

North American Indians Scraping Hide
Studying traditional crafts helps us understand how the same tasks may have been done in the past.
COURTESY OF CAROLINE WICKHAM-JONES

middens were occupied so regularly at different seasons. Different groups could have had traditional rights to go to exploit the shellfish on Oronsay at different times of year.

Bevel-ended Tools

Bevel-ended tools appear as a very simple form of artefact. They are made of bone, antler or stone, and are quite long with a bevelled end. The tools have often been described as limpet hammers (generally when made of stone) and limpet scoops (generally when made of bone or antler). What they were really used for is another matter and serves to illustrate the development of archaeological ideas through debate and also shows how such simple pieces of evidence can begin to play an important role in our understanding of past behaviour.

I have suggested that these tools may have been used for leather working. A colleague at Edinburgh University, Clive Bonsall, argues that the tools are used as limpet hammers, and that their form is the result of their use in collecting the limpets that are common in some middens. Both of us have some experimental data to show that our interpretations are at least possible. Clive has advanced the argument that the association of bone and antler bevel-ended tools with the midden sites supports his case. I have argued that these tools are preserved here by the soil chemistry produced in the middens, and that stone examples are often found away from midden sites, suggesting that the presence of the bone and antler examples is an accident of preservation, rather than a consequence of how they were used. There are

cases, best known in Cornwall, where these bevel-ended tools are not associated with shell middens, but are always found away from the midden sites. Tools with similar bevelled ends are known from other parts of the world, both in north-west America and in Australia, and in all these cases they are used for leather working, both for softening the material and for smoothing seams. Research being conducted while this book was being written has given greater support to Clive's argument, as an analysis of the

microscopic traces on some of the bone and antler tools suggests that they were not used for leather working.

The significance of the disagreement is that Clive's theory sees the tools as firmly placed within the food economy (whether the limpets were being collected to be eaten or used for bait), whereas my suggestion places the tools in the context of understanding social issues, as tools being used to produce well-made clothing.

Bevel-ended Tool Forms
NATIONAL MUSEUMS OF SCOTLAND

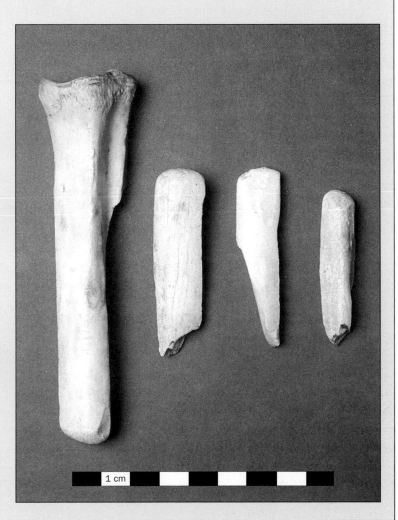

1 cm

Who made the middens?

One of the apparent problems of the Scottish Mesolithic has
been why midden sites are so different from other types of site.
Most other sites are dominated by collections of stone tools,
including forms called microliths which are not found in the
middens. I will describe these in Chapter 4. One of the most
interesting recent discoveries has been the site of An Corran on
Skye, found by chance during road building, where shell midden
artefacts were found mixed with microliths. This confirms
information from excavations many years ago on the little island
of Risga in Loch Sunart, where a microlith was found
apparently associated with the midden. Unfortunately
the excavation records made at that time did not
make it clear if the midden had just accumulated
where someone had previously dropped a
microlith hundreds of years before. Finding
the microliths and the
midden together is very
important, as at one
time archaeologists
thought that the
people who left
middens were a separate,
later culture. They called
this the 'Obanian' after a
series of middens found
around Oban. The
Obanian was seen
as a late stage of the
Mesolithic, separate from
the microlith-making
stage. Nowadays we see
the middens as simply
representing one aspect of
Mesolithic life, where a different
tool kit was required. This new
interpretation is to a great extent based
on the employment of a new scientific
development, where much smaller samples of organic remains
can be subject to radiocarbon dating. This not only allows
smaller remains to be dated, but means that tools can be dated
by taking very small samples without having to destroy an
entire artefact.

As with all new discoveries, this revelation required a re-
examination of the Obanian. The absence of antler and bone

Hide Working
Many traditional chores have always
served as social activities.
HARRY BLAND

Raschoille Cave

One of the small caves in the Oban cliffs.
Unfortunately there is often little to see at
these sites nowadays. Here access to the
cave has had to be restricted as the roof is
unsafe.

CAROLINE WICKHAM-JONES

tools away from the midden sites could be explained by the fact
that these materials are only preserved because the shell-rich
middens provide the right chemical conditions for preservation.
It was, however, difficult to explain why no one had ever taken
a microlith to a shell midden site and lost it there. An Corran has
brought the two types of evidence together. Archaeologist Tony
Pollard has now gone back to the site of Risga – or what is left
of it – and has discovered that next to the midden is a microlith-
rich site. This illustrates two points: firstly, that so far we have
only excavated a small number of Mesolithic sites, and our
knowledge is so patchy that every new excavation is likely to
throw up interesting results; secondly, that in the past
archaeologists have excavated middens and because of the good
preservation within the midden, have never looked beyond the
midden, to find out if there are other discoveries to be made
nearby.

Mesolithic Boats

We know from settlements on islands such as Rhum, Colonsay, Skye and Islay and from the fish bones found on their sites, that Mesolithic people in Scotland were successful seafarers. What we are not sure about is how they travelled between islands. There appear to have been two means, one being the coracle, a lightweight frame covered with leather, the other being a canoe made from a log. No examples of either have been found recently to allow them to be dated by modern techniques such as radiocarbon dating. Coracles, because of their lightweight nature, are the more perishable of the two, and none have been discovered. There have been some examples of dugout canoes found, mostly during peat cutting last century, but none survive. Some of these appear to be more recent than the Mesolithic, but other examples may have been Mesolithic. At present, the balance of evidence suggests that Mesolithic waters were travelled by canoe. The examples found, however, have mostly come from freshwater locations, such as former lochs and lakes, and we do not know if these vessels would have been up to crossing stretches of open sea. My guess is that they would have been. They represent a considerable amount of work, and it appears unlikely that this technology would have been adopted if coracles were in regular use at sea.

Canoe and Coracle Manufacture
HARRY BLAND

Gathering Hazels

The illustration shows people harvesting
hazel shells to take back to their camp.
Roasted hazelnuts may have been an
important form of stored food for times
when fresh resources were scarce.
Gathering plant foods will have
been important, and will have
mostly been done by women.
HARRY BLAND

Life in the Woods

The crowd of children were busy collecting the nuts that were falling from the trees onto the skins laid out underneath. Some of the women were already starting to carry baskets full of nuts back to the camp. From beyond the clearing where the hazels grew, rising above the thick woods that lay between them and the campsite, the smoke could already be seen rising from the fires in the roasting pits where the nuts would be cooked. This was a busy time of year for everyone, as the nuts had to be gathered and processed for storage so that they could be eaten throughout the winter months ahead, when other foods were scarce.

Over the last few years evidence has been steadily accumulating of the deliberate management of the woods that would have covered much of Scotland during the Mesolithic. Most of the direct evidence we have is not from traditional archaeology, but from palynology, the study of pollen (see p.32). We have always known that because hunter-gatherers were so dependent on and involved with their environment that it is very important to establish what that environment was. Palynologists study the evidence for past environments and given the many changes that people have made to the environment in Scotland since they first arrived, the reconstructions that they can make are vital. What is more, we must remember that climate has changed since the Mesolithic. Hunter-gatherers first moved into Scotland not long after the ice sheets of the last glaciation retreated. By the time in which we are interested, when there appears to have been a permanent and significant occupation of Scotland, the climate was somewhat warmer than it is today.

In the past, the work of people interested in the ancient environment was regarded merely as background material by archaeologists trying to

Staosnaig Excavations
Steven Mithen's excavations at Staosnaig on Colonsay have recovered a scatter of stone tools and pits, including a large pit which seems to be full of all sorts plant refuse, including many hazel shells. This is extremely important as such remains are very rarely preserved from the Mesolithic. The polythene greenhouse allows careful excavation work to carry on regardless of the weather.
CAROLINE WICKHAM-JONES

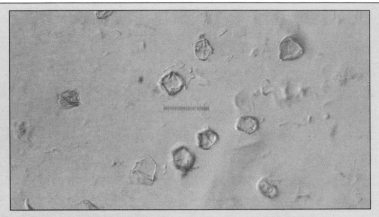

Pollen Grains of Hazel and Alder
Hazel was an important plant food in the Mesolithic.
MIKE CRESSEY

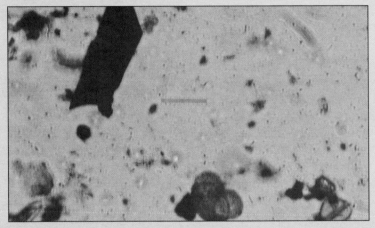

Pollen Grains of Pine with Fragments of Microscopic Charcoal
Such charcoal fragments may be the remains of Mesolithic woodland management.
MIKE CRESSEY

Core Sample
This is a column of peat and soil which has just been collected from a site on Coll.
GERAINT COLES

Pollen Analysis

Pollen analysts (palynologists) identify pollen grains that are preserved in sediments to reconstruct vegetation patterns and changes over time. The best pollen records occur in peat or lake deposits, where the absence of oxygen helps to preserve the pollen grains and the pollen is preserved in a relatively static environment. This means that pollen accumulates pretty much at the same time as the sediments, giving us a column from which samples can be taken in thin slices representing different periods.

In essence this is a straightforward process. A column of peat or lake muds is taken, usually as a core, so that the sequence of growth of the peat or deposition of the muds can be seen. This relies on the same basic principle of stratigraphy upon which much archaeological excavation depends, where more recent material lies on top of older material. By taking slices from these columns and examining the range and frequency of pollen within these slices, pollen analysis can obtain a great deal of information, including information on climate changes (very important when we are interested as a period as far back in time as the Mesolithic) and information on deliberate changes to the vegetation, for example those caused by forest clearance, as well as simply what was growing in the area. There are, of course, all sorts of difficulties, but pollen analysis has become one of the most important ways of understanding this aspect of the early past.

establish the resources available to the first hunter-gatherers. The picture has not remained so simple, however. It now appears clear that from very early on people were modifying their environment; this was, at least to begin with, a rather controversial discovery. Hunter-gatherers were supposed to live a non-intrusive lifestyle, almost as one with the wild, as creatures that were part of the environment. It was generally assumed that it was only when farmers came along and chopped down trees and ploughed fields that people had a significant impact on their surroundings. It now appears clear that hunter-gatherers too were altering their surroundings. This modification would probably nowadays be called management, in the way that a modern park ranger or conservation manager might look after a woodland to encourage certain sorts of rare species to flourish, rather than direct control of an environment, but they were clearly interfering. One of the most obvious traces of this is in the establishment of clearings in woods. We have been able to identify localised clearing of the woods from evidence in cores taken for pollen analysis.

One of the most spectacular discoveries concerning Mesolithic use of woodland resources has been made recently by archaeologist Steve Mithen and his team at the site of Staosnaig on Colonsay. Here, at a site on the old beach a pit has been

Charred Hazel Shells
These are the most common plant remains to survive, but this is probably the result of a preservation bias, as most other plant remains will decay very rapidly.
CAROLINE WICKHAM-JONES

1 cm

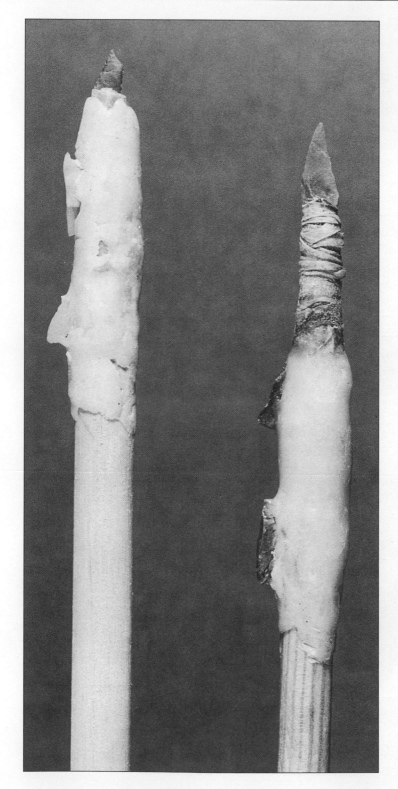

Microliths

Microliths (literally 'small stones') are a very common type of find across much of Europe and the Middle East and date from late in the last Ice Age until the beginning of farming. They are small, generally only a few centimetres long, and sometimes tiny, less than a centimetre long. They are made of long, thin flakes of flint produced by a sophisticated technique designed to produce a large number of fairly standard usable pieces from each flint pebble. They come in a range of shapes, many being geometric forms, such as scalene triangles, crescents, and trapezes. Some of the fine needle-like pointed tools are very well made. A whole range of functions has been ascribed to them, including their use as tattooing needles, drill bits, inserts for sickles, the tips and barbs of arrows, and as elements of graters and other plant processing tools. For a while in western Europe their possible use as the tips and barbs of arrows was the most popular theory, but there is evidence to suggest that other uses were common too. Some archaeologists pointed out that similar tools were, until recently, still used in some parts of the tropics for plant processing, or as fishing equipment. There has been a considerable amount of argument about this, but recent studies of the patterns of microscopic traces of damage

Tool Reconstruction
These arrows were made for experimental use so that the microscopic traces that were then left on the tools could be looked at and then compared with archaeological material.
BILL FINLAYSON

on the tools have shown that they were probably used in all sorts of different ways.

This has formed an important part of the debate about how important hunting was, and how important stone tools were, to Mesolithic people. Based on the use of microliths in arrows, one French archaeologist described the Mesolithic as the period of archery hunting. Other people have tried to identify different communities in the Mesolithic on the basis of different microlith shapes, believing that arrowheads are a very visible tool and that given the importance of hunting, this would be a good way to announce which tribe you belonged to. Unfortunately, most microliths are too small to be very visible, and by the time they had been stuck into a wooden haft (which would have required a socket, and some adhesive materials, such as a mix of resin and beeswax, perhaps also with some binding), not enough would be left sticking out to be useful as a way of letting people know where you were from!

Furthermore, we should not overemphasise how important stone was to the Mesolithic – they may have seen these little bits of flint as very small components of their tools, and have been far more worried about the wooden haft that would have taken much longer to make, but which does not survive for us to study. Most archaeologists looking at the Scottish Mesolithic now suspect that microliths were the world's first plug-in tool replacement part, and that as stone edges wore out, they were thrown away and new ones put in place.

Microliths
A range of fairly typical Scottish microliths.
JOE ROCK, UNIVERSITY OF EDINBURGH

1 cm

found, possibly excavated for a house or shelter. When this structure was abandoned, the pit was filled up with hazel shells. The number of shells is so large that every piece has not been counted, but estimates suggest that hundreds of thousands of hazel shells were dumped into this pit. A microscopic analysis of the pit contents made by a soil scientist has shown that the shells were all dumped at about the same time, in other words during the same harvesting season. This number of shells represents a fantastic harvest and a huge amount of harvesting.

What can have been going on? Steve Mithen has looked at a number of possibilities, and using expert advice from botanists and the evidence from experiments undertaken by his students, has come up with a possible explanation. Around the big pit are a number of smaller pits, and it seems likely that the harvesters were roasting their nuts to help store them. Indeed, once they were roasted they may have gone on to make a paste that would take up far less space that the whole nut kernels. Roasting also improves the flavour of the nuts.

Colonsay may have been a particularly good place to harvest nuts, since, as far as we know, there have never been any squirrels on the island, so eliminating one of the main competitors for the nuts. Even still, the number of nuts harvested is huge, and this may be more evidence that Mesolithic people were not only collecting from wild resources, but were managing them. By burning out clearings in woods they may have

Microlith Manufacture
We don't know whether everyone made stone tools, or whether it was left to experts. In any event, it must have been a craft that was passed on by the elders of the community.
HARRY BLAND

encouraged hazel growth. To increase the harvest still more they may have been pruning the trees, a likely activity given that there is some evidence from Europe that Mesolithic people were actively managing trees by coppicing and pollarding – pruning to encourage the growth of long, straight branches with few knots.

Not only does the harvest suggest woodland management, but it also suggests that a considerable number of people must have been assembled to gather and process all the nuts. The nut harvest and processing may have been an occasion for a number of groups to congregate. The location of this site on Colonsay is interesting, given the nearby middens on Oronsay, but perhaps we should not exaggerate this connection, as it is more likely to be an accident of preservation. Perhaps instead we should think that there may have been many such sites around Scotland.

The most common Mesolithic tool that we find nowadays is the microlith (see p.34). Microliths are typical of most Mesolithic sites away from the shell middens, whether they are up in the hills or down by the coast. They are used as the quickest and surest way of deciding whether a site is Mesolithic or not. People produced vast numbers of microliths, and much of the other chipped stone on Mesolithic sites may be the waste products produced while making these tools. Other stone tools were made, including tools for scraping hides and for shaving wood. These are generally all called scrapers. Unfortunately, people continued to make scrapers after the Mesolithic, and although there are some types that appear to be restricted to particular periods, most could belong to any period of stone tool use.

Excavating most Mesolithic sites involves a considerable amount of time spent collecting the stone needed for tool manufacture. The materials used vary, the most well known being flint, but other materials such as chert and volcanic rocks such as pitchstone from Arran and bloodstone from Rhum have all been used. These stone tools can tell us a great deal about a site and the people who occupied it. We can get an idea of the range of tasks they carried out from the range of tools that are present; for example a tool manufacturing site can be identified from the amount of stone rubbish left. We can see where these people collected their stone by looking for the sources of the stones being used. Looking at sites such as Smittons and Starr in the Galloway Hills and comparing them with the sites down by the coast, both on the west in Ayrshire and to the south along the Solway Firth, we have begun to be able to estimate the movement patterns of these people, who probably travelled from the coast into the hills at different times of the year to exploit different resources. We will explore why hunter-gatherers moved from site to site in the next chapter.

Loch Doon

When the water level was low a series of
Mesolithic sites was found here where the
normal water level had eroded the peat.
Other sites have been found in a similar
manner elsewhere in southern Scotland,
and indicate that the inland hills may have
been extensively occupied, although the
sites are normally hard to find.
CAROLINE WICKHAM-JONES

Making Choices

The group sat together around the fire. The boy's uncle was complaining that he had not caught anything for several days, and although his aunt had teased him that this was because he was getting too fat and everyone had laughed, everyone had agreed and then fallen silent.

After a while the old man let out a long sigh and said perhaps it was time to move on. For a while everyone sat nodding in agreement, looking down at the fire. His wife suggested they should move into the next valley, for the berries would be ripening now and could be picked. The old man, glad to have a chance to get his own back, said that this was a silly idea. His hunting had taken him into the valley and there was no sign that there would be many berries there this year; besides the old man's sister's children had been through that valley just recently and had probably chased off much of the game. A lively discussion followed until gradually they all agreed on the best course of action. They were to split up until the autumn meeting, when the group would join with others to harvest the autumn fruits and salmon to store for the winter.

The boy was cheered up by the thought of the autumn gathering. There were always plenty of people to play with then and strangers to meet. If only they didn't have to split up till then. When he was with just his family, there were fewer chances to play and his father made him work harder.

Hunter-gatherers had a lot of choices to make during the course of their year, but many of these choices were limited by the seasons and the resources available at different times. An important point about humans is that faced by an environment, we can choose how we wish to behave. One of the most interesting things about hunter-gatherer archaeology is trying to work out how people thought about things in the past, and one of the best ways to start to do this is to see if we can understand how they organised themselves.

There are a number of basic ways in which people can organise themselves. The simplest, and the one that we seem to share with our ape relations, is to live in small groups and wander through an area from resource to resource, moving on as each area becomes depleted. Early hominids probably lived like this. It is perhaps easiest in the tropics, where the availability of natural foods may not vary enormously between seasons. It is not so good in a climate like ours, as the seasons may cause big changes in the availability of foods – for example there are few animals to hunt in the hills in the winter, plant foods run out in the autumn, while fish and birds may migrate.

Probably the first major modification to this lifestyle is to design a seasonal round, so that the wanderings through the landscape become more structured. A common and simple

model for Mesolithic Scotland has been that people scattered into small groups in the summer and went to hunt in the hills. In the winter they moved down to the coast and relied on marine resources such as fish and shellfish.

A further adaptation is to have a home camp (often called a base camp), where at least some people live all year. This has the great advantage that you do not have to keep moving around all the time, carrying all your goods, foods and small children with you. Unfortunately, if you are relying on natural resources, you run the risk that you will eat everything within reach and run out of food. Obviously, the more food resources around your

Tanged Points

These flint tools from Scotland look identical to tools called Ahrensburgian Points found in northern Europe and dating to before 10,000 years ago. At present they appear to be the earliest evidence for the human colonisation of Scotland.

JOE ROCK, UNIVERSITY OF EDINBURGH

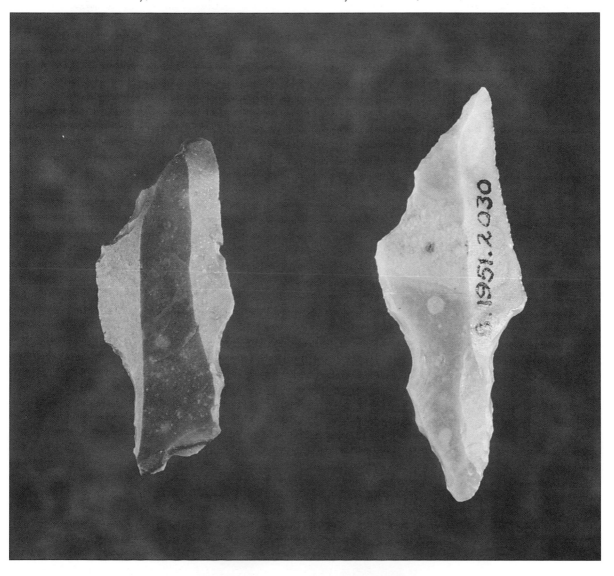

1 cm

A Gathering
When people met up in
larger groups, this would
have been an occasion for
celebration. Old relations
would have met with each other,
while some of the younger members
of the groups would have been trying to
meet partners from outside their
immediate family group.
HARRY BLAND

home camp at the start, the longer they will last. This can be helped even more if some of the resources come to you at different times of the year, for example in seasonal migrations, such as with salmon, geese, deer, and so on, or in seasonal availability, such as the ripening of berries and nuts. Unfortunately, there are few places where such year-long abundance is reliable. There are other problems too. If you live in one place all the time, you will start to use up all the available firewood. If people do not get on with each other, but have to carry on living with each other, you may find that arguments

Narrow Blade Microliths
These are the tools that are the most commonly found distinctive evidence for the Scottish Mesolithic.
JOE ROCK, UNIVERSITY OF EDINBURGH

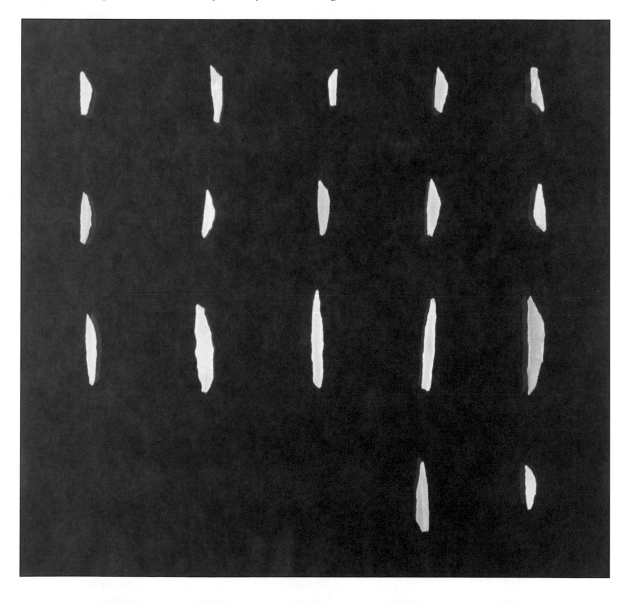

1 cm

become more and more frequent. If something goes wrong with any particular resource that is crucial to feed the community at one time of year, the whole system can collapse.

The base camp idea can be modified too. It is possible to combine some of the benefits of the base camp with those of the seasonal round by using a base camp, but sending out small parties as work groups. These parties can head off to other locations where at certain times of year particular resources are known to be plentiful, and they can then bring back the fruits of their work to the base camp. Work parties could also keep in touch with other groups, keeping the community informed of a larger area and allowing some trading of goods and information.

Where does the Scottish Mesolithic fit into this? Well, it is unlikely that over the period we are interested in any one system would have stayed the same all the time. We can expect some change over time. The evidence is quite interesting.

Early visitors to Scotland

In the earliest part of the Mesolithic in Scotland we see only a few artefacts scattered around. There are no proper sites, just stray tools, of a type called the Ahrensburgian Point, very similar to those found in northern Europe and dating to before 10,000 years ago. They are scattered quite widely over the north and west of Scotland, from Orkney round to Tiree, Islay and Jura. These tools are very distinctive, so we can be fairly sure that the people who made them are part of the same society as that seen in Europe, and therefore of the same period. Archaeologists have argued that if this is the case, we should be finding proper sites, or perhaps that the sites now lie submerged under the sea which has risen since then. I think that this is wrong. We have not found proper sites, despite looking for them. At the same time, it seems unlikely that all of these early people's camps were on the shore. My interpretation is that we see a few scattered tools because of the way people first arrived here. The tools are the remains of small parties of people moving across the landscape who do not establish long-term or large camp sites. Given their distribution around coastal areas, it is possible that what we are seeing are the traces of small hunting parties moving rapidly by boat.

The next phase of the Mesolithic in Scotland is characterised by a particular type of tool, the broad blade microlith. Again there are very few sites, but now the evidence is for proper sites. These people were camping, but perhaps not for long, and there were not many of them. It again appears most likely that we are dealing with people travelling across the landscape with no fixed bases.

The colonisation of Scotland

The next period is quite different. People started to make
narrow blade microliths and at the same time seem to have
started to settle in Scotland in a much more substantial way. Sites
such as Kinloch Farm on Rhum, and Bolsay Farm on Islay, yield
hundreds of thousands of bits of flint tools and manufacturing
waste. There are pits, holes for stakes, and evidence for hearths.
Unfortunately, it is hard to determine whether these sites relate
to long periods of occupation, or regular visits every year for
short periods over a long time. Either way, we now appear to
have people doing something systematically different from what
has happened before. It would appear that they had either
developed structured seasonal rounds, where they return to the
same place on a regular basis, or that they had established base
camps.

There does not, as yet, appear to be the sort of evidence to
show that these base camps were permanently occupied. If they
were, I am sure we would have begun to find evidence for

San Camps
Many hunter-gatherer camps are so slight
that we may never find evidence for them.
ALAN BARNARD

better, more solid structures. The islands of the west coast of Scotland are located within a very rich environment, with all sorts of changing resources in the form of fish and migratory birds, so it would have been technically possible to have established a base camp system, but such a system tends to develop a greater degree of social complexity than we see evidence for. Some evidence for this of course may not have been preserved, or has not been found, but if we compare this area with the north-west coast of America, where settled hunter-gatherers did become established, we can see huge differences. This was brought home to me by a Canadian archaeologist, Rick Schulting, who introduced me to the enormously rich material culture of the recent north-west coast American Indians, who carved massive ornate and fantastic totem poles, lived in large substantial houses, and even kept slaves. Our hunter-gatherers were a long way from this. Equally, they were a long way from the highly mobile people of marginal environments, such as the Kalahari Desert.

I think that our people had begun to develop the base camp idea during the Mesolithic period in Scotland. Certainly some of the evidence points to it. As well as these large sites, there are also small flint scatter sites, where the evidence suggests that small numbers of people occupied sites for short periods. One such site lies close to Bolsay Farm at Gleann Mor, and it is tempting to see this as a camp site belonging to a work party from Bolsay Farm. Other sites in other parts of Scotland help to fill in the patterns of movement. There are sites in the Galloway hills, such as Smittons and Starr, which are generally small, and probably represent hunting camps. We should not just think in terms of deer hunting, however: Scottish rivers and lochs provide a considerable resource from fishing and wildfowling, and many of the sites along rivers such as the Tweed are the result of small bands who probably moved up and down the rivers. Water transport is likely to have been an important factor in movement patterns, as otherwise the only way to transport belongings, food and small children would have been to carry them.

Comparable evidence from the final stages of the Mesolithic in northern Europe suggests that the base camp idea was evolving there too. Evidence from Denmark points to large base camps with enormous shell middens, the use of pottery (which, given its heavy and breakable nature, suggests people were not moving around very much), and to small task camps. The latter are very clear, as there are a number of camps where people seem to have gone to intercept migrating resources, such as dolphins or swans, and to have only occupied these sites to exploit these very short-term resources.

Wildwoods
This misty image may be more of a reflection of the landscape our Mesolithic forbears saw than the open expanses of much of modern Scotland. However, this rather romantic view is a modern image. Hunter-gatherers will have known every corner of their environment in great detail to allow them to survive on the wild resources present.
GERAINT COLES

This pattern may have continued to develop through the final stages of the Mesolithic in Scotland too. Nearly all of our surviving shell middens appear to be very late in the Mesolithic. Some, such as Ulva Cave on Ulva off the Isle of Mull, probably continued in use during the early farming period, and perhaps even longer. The presence of groups of middens on Oronsay and around Oban, which mostly appear to have been used during the same period, suggests an intensification of resource use, where groups perhaps may no longer have been quite so free to move due to population pressure. Alternatively, or as part of the same process, people may have been restructuring their economies to rely more and more on predictable marine resources, and less on high-risk hunting.

We may even see a continuity into the early farming period in the west of Scotland. The middens continued in use, but no villages appeared, suggesting that groups of people remained at least partially mobile. What did appear are burial cairns (and later on, burials in middens) and these elaborate funerary structures have often been interpreted as marking land ownership. If people are using particular resources more and more intensively, they do not have to start farming to mark out their own resources. Equally, farming on the west coast and islands may have been adopted only gradually by the local Mesolithic people. The rugged landscape may not have been very suitable for early farming practice, while the rich marine environment and its relatively abundant food resources may have meant that people were unwilling to commence the hard work associated with farming.

At Sea's Edge
The west coast of Scotland provides a wide variety of environments within a small area. These would have provided a range of different resources for hunter-gatherers, reducing the need to travel.
IAN RALSTON

Behaviour and Belief

The young mother had died in the night. Although such things happened all too often, the family were grief-stricken. She had appeared so strong and healthy. Some of the other women in the group now had charge of arranging her body for burial and were gathering together her favourite tools: the carved wooden haft which her grandmother had given her, re-used again and again for new stone knife blades; the leather water bag which she had made for herself in the autumn; and several strings of shells which her man had given her.

It had fallen to the oldest women to wrap up the stillborn baby to keep it warm for the next world.

The men and children stood a short way off, not wanting to interfere, not wanting to get too close. This was not their time and not their place, but in the small group they wanted to show their support for the women, and they felt their grief. The young woman's man squatted down, his face streaked dark with ash from the cold fireplace. Even the dogs sat uneasily, whining quietly.

Burials can tell us a great deal about how people viewed the world around them. Unfortunately, we have no direct evidence of burial from the Scottish Mesolithic. There are Mesolithic burials elsewhere in Europe, notably in southern Scandinavia, the eastern Baltic and Portugal. These show a tremendously rich variety in burial practice – and include some startling examples, such as a baby lying on a swan's wing next to its mother, a man and woman buried together, dog burials, and people buried upright in vertical shafts. People are buried with pierced animal teeth used as beads, resting on antlers, and even some with arrowheads embedded in their bodies, suggesting a violent end.

We do not know where Mesolithic burial sites might be found in Scotland. The combination of mainly acidic soils, patterns of sea level change, and the accidents of preservation may well hide a burial tradition as rich as in mainland Europe. This is a shame, as burials provide so much data on people, not only from the skeletal evidence that lets us see how healthy a population was, but also from the insights they can provide on social structure and ideology. That said, perhaps we can use the knowledge that Mesolithic burials exist to provide us with a general framework of the sort of behaviour that may have been current during the Mesolithic. Burial sites are not the same throughout Europe, and vary over time, so there is no point in examining them in any detail as each local situation would clearly have been different. However, it is clear that societies had developed where the dead were respected, and where the relationships between man and woman and mother and baby

were acknowledged. While we cannot say what exactly the symbolism represented by a baby buried on a swan's wing means, we can infer that these people had a poetic, symbolic side to their lives. Burying dogs and burying people upright also suggests complexities in their lives. It has been suggested that upright burials might have been for priests or shaman, and that dog burials might represent the burials of priests whose spirits had moved into animals after their own deaths. This last interpretation, based on ethnographic analogy, is a good reminder that we must not look at societies just with our own eyes, where we might have been inclined to believe that they buried their favourite dogs out of sentimentality.

Within this world of Mesolithic symbolism, what can we tell about how people in Scotland behaved? We have seen how rich the Scottish Mesolithic is in economic data, but is there anything we can say about society without burial evidence?

Clothing and personal decoration can tell us a lot about society. Clothing is an important issue. Generally, people can survive without much clothing, except in extreme climates such as arctic or sub-arctic zones. There are examples of people, such as the Andaman islanders, who lived in similar temperature ranges to Scotland, who survived with very crude capes. If we can accept that the bevel-ended tools may have been used for leather working, this would allow us to argue that considerable efforts were being put into making leather goods. From the Scottish shell middens we have a large number of pierced cowrie shells. The general assumption is that these would have been strung together as necklaces. There are no examples of strung beads from Scotland, but Scandinavian burials provide some indications of how they may have been put together, and these seem to have been as fairly elaborate head-dresses, or possibly as skirts, and not as simple strings of beads. Once again, because we are looking at the Mesolithic, we tend to suggest that everything would have been very basic but we must remember that these were people with brains just like ours. In north-west America the Indians made very elaborate leather clothing. The cowrie shell beads would suggest that the Scottish Mesolithic people were interested in personal decoration and certainly if the bevel-ended tools were used for leather working, a lot of leather working was going on. In north-west America, the production of fine leather clothes was a way of demonstrating wealth. The Indian men were able to demonstrate that they were rich in that they had enough wives for some of the wives to spend their time on the manufacture of luxury goods, rather than just on subsistence.

There are other, stranger, details in some of the shell middens. Paul Mellars' excavations on Oronsay recovered

Burial
In the illustration are a number of images taken from known burial sites in southern Scandinavia. Corpses were often laid on antlers, mothers were sometimes buried with their babies (presumably if the mother had died giving birth), people were buried with their beads, and sometimes tools were placed in the grave with them. The priest or shaman is wearing a set of antlers – we know from sets found in England that antlers were probably worn.
HARRY BLAND

BEHAVIOUR AND BELIEF 51

evidence for numbers of human finger bones buried within the middens. We do not know how they got there. Some people have suggested that they got their by accident, as the inclusion of general material from settlements. It is possible that people in Scotland did not bury their dead, at least not immediately, and that this is why we have found no graves. This may sound a little strange, but exposing bodies to the elements, to allow them to rot, or be scavenged by birds, often as a first stage before burial, is a practice that we know from various places around the world. Some North American Indians did this, placing their dead on raised platforms. Evidence from early farming (Neolithic) communities in Britain has suggested that they may have used the same practice. Similar rites are still followed by the Parsees in India. Such a practice might explain the absence of graves, and might also explain how small bones might accidentally end up scattered in a midden — such bones are small and easily lost once the flesh that holds them together has gone.

Such an explanation would be acceptable, were it not for the fact that some of the finger bones appear to have been deliberately placed on top of seal flippers within the middens. This immediately raises the possibility of the bones providing some intriguing evidence for ideas about burial, death, and indeed life. We can only guess at what significance was attached to such acts, but they not only show a greater concern for human remains, but also perhaps indicate that the shell middens, which we have traditionally interpreted simply as food waste, had other roles in life. Placing human fingers on top of a flipper in a midden suggests that the midden was a special place. The people who used these middens may not have seen a sharp boundary between holy and everyday. Nowadays we recognise a difference between a grave which is symbolic and a midden which is economic. Mesolithic people may not have seen this boundary. People may have buried their dead assuming that after dying life went on in pretty much the same way somewhere else, which is why they buried people with belongings and in their families. Equally, people may have seen their own living world as full of spirits, not just as a mundane and rational place. Australian aborigines see their landscape as rich in special places, a living thing with which they interact, rather than a passive object they use. Indeed, they go further and it is hard for westerners to appreciate fully the way they perceive the landscape and their visions of the dreamtime. Archaeologist Tony Pollard has argued that we need to spend more time thinking

about such spiritual and symbolic aspects of the Mesolithic in Scotland, as without appreciating that such activities would have been essential to the people we are studying, we can never hope to make sense of their lives.

Again, however, it is important, not to simply take known aspects of the modern world and put them into the past. 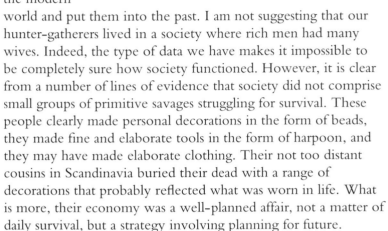 I am not suggesting that our hunter-gatherers lived in a society where rich men had many wives. Indeed, the type of data we have makes it impossible to be completely sure how society functioned. However, it is clear from a number of lines of evidence that society did not comprise small groups of primitive savages struggling for survival. These people clearly made personal decorations in the form of beads, they made fine and elaborate tools in the form of harpoon, and they may have made elaborate clothing. Their not too distant cousins in Scandinavia buried their dead with a range of decorations that probably reflected what was worn in life. What is more, their economy was a well-planned affair, not a matter of daily survival, but a strategy involving planning for future.

Modern clues to the past

One problem we face is the difficulty of imagining the viewpoint of humans several thousand years ago. Nowadays we have a huge amount of information about how other people think, from books, television, and from the ease with which modern people can travel and mix. One of the most striking observations that can be made is just how differently some societies view the world. We need not look at modern hunter-gatherers; the differences between different urban cultures, such as between the modern Japanese and, say, the Italians, are obvious. Importantly, if you think about many of the obvious things we share in common, you can see that these are recent, the products of a general world culture that has been developing since the Second World War. Modern communications, cheap air travel, the telephone, television, cinema, the giant multi-national companies that try to sell the same goods around the world, have all contributed to reducing the differences between cultures. However, even now there are differences, differences often used for example in comedy, where we can laugh at the strange things foreigners do. Now start to think back into the past. It is not that long ago that few people ever travelled far. At the start of this century most people took their holidays in their

Harpoons
Mesolithic harpoons are substantial tools that would have required a considerable effort to manufacture and this investment in time must have been matched by their effectiveness.
NATIONAL MUSEUMS OF SCOTLAND

Mesolithic Landscape
Archaeologists often spend most
of their time looking at individual sites.
It is important, especially during the Mesolithic
when we are studying mobile societies, to look at the
entire landscape. Hunter gatherers will have used every
part of it they could, perhaps hunting in the uplands,
collecting plant foods in the hills and fishing on the coast.
HARRY BLAND

own country. Foreigners really were exotic. Only a few hundred years ago people believed in races of people with only a single eye, or other such stories. Go back several thousands of years and think of the Egyptians, whose religion and burial practices are now the stuff of legend. Yet the Egyptians may well be closer to us in some ways than the hunter-gatherers of Scotland. The Egyptians lived in settled communities, they ate farm produce, they had a government, an army, officials. To get to our hunter-gatherers we have to go back almost twice as far in time.

So, how useful is it to look at modern hunter-gatherers as a way of understanding the past? The trouble with modern hunter-gatherers is that many of them have now been in contact with other cultures for a long time. African hunter-gatherers, for example, were first in contact with farming Africans, and since then have been part of the modern countries that they live in. Modern hunter-gatherers often live in close relationships with settled populations, often trading with them, providing animal herders or a seasonal labour force. They have had 10,000 years to change from the period we are interested in. However, if we can see any general patterns of thought, perhaps these can give us insights into how people may have seen the world.

Kinloch Farm, Rhum
Excavation in process at the site of Kinloch Farm on the island of Rhum. Caroline Wickham-Jones' excavations here sparked off a new wave of Mesolithic research in Scotland.
CAROLINE WICKHAM-JONES

On a calm day it is easy to imagine
Mesolithic people travelling between the
islands of the southern Hebrides in canoes.
IAN RALSTON

One thing that is clear is that most modern hunter-gatherers
do not fully share our way of thinking about where they fit into
the world. We tend to divide the world into natural and man-
made. We see the world as a series of opposites – town and
country, tame and wild. All sorts of ideas are bound up in this.
The controlled, man-made situation is generally seen as safe; the
untamed wild world is seen as dangerous. Much of this is an
illusion, since most of our countryside is of course the result of
thousands of years of farming and forestry, and many wild places
are far safer than many man-made places, such as roads. It is,
however, the way that we view the world. Hunter-gatherers do
not see this same divide. In a sense, many of them see themselves
as part of the world, part of what we might describe as nature.
They do not see themselves in a controlling position.

Hunter-gatherers generally do not have the same ideas about
property as most settled societies do. They put less work into
developing resources, they do not clear land, cultivate it, sow it,
weed it, water it, and so on to harvest a crop. Even where they

BEHAVIOUR AND BELIEF 57

Island Landscape

Many of the landscapes we find hunter-gatherer sites in appear wild. However this wilderness is a modern creation, often caused by a combination of sheep grazing and climate change. In the Mesolithic much more of the landscape would have been covered with trees and scrub, providing shelter, food and the raw materials for making artefacts.

IAN RALSTON

do intervene in the environment to improve harvests, the investment of effort and time is far less than for farmers. Hunter-gatherers have traditional resources, but they are generally less exclusive, and do not revolve around the idea of ownership.

Mesolithic hunter-gatherers probably had quite a lot of spare time, at least for some of the year. Many modern hunter-gatherers spend a fair amount of time resting. Harvesting wild resources may not support the same number of people as farming, but if you know how to do it, it is easier!

They would be familiar with only small groups of people – during their whole lives they might not meet any more than a few hundred individuals – no more than you might see at a school or in a big supermarket.

All modern hunter-gatherers generally seem to share resources. There may be complicated rules as to who gets what and how much, but it is commonplace amongst hunter-gatherers to share food. Many peoples also share other items. In this type of situation theft is rare. There may be a practical reason for

sharing. With wild resources there is a good chance that you will have a bad day hunting or that the grove of trees you visit may not have any fruit on it. Sharing reduces the risks you face, as it is unlikely everyone in the group will have had the same poor luck. When people hunt big animals they often do not manage to catch one every day, but when they do, there is more than enough food for everyone. By sharing with others at the base camp you get food when you do not have any, and supply food when you do. This principle also allows hunter-gatherers to look after anyone who is not well enough to forage, or who has had an accident.

Most hunter-gatherers live in roughly egalitarian societies and have no chiefs. No one is forced to do anything. If one does not like what the group is doing, they can leave. Of course, if you do leave, and if you do not cooperate and share, then you expose yourself to greater risks. Many social conventions may well have been developed to reduce risks, for example it is common for hunter-gatherers to marry outside their band. This helps to ensure that they have friends and relations in other parts of the country, and this may come in handy in times of local hardship when they want to move beyond their normal range. Most hunter-gatherer societies have all sorts of ways they keep in touch with people over long distances, and these can include meeting up during times of plenty for parties, gift-giving and ritual activities. Many of our current social activities probably originate with these.

One common assumption has been that of an ancient division of labour by sex, men hunting and women gathering plant foods. This pattern is largely based on traditional ethnographic analogies with tropical hunter-gatherers where plant foods are possibly the most important food resource. They also relate to our modern conception of hunting as an activity involving big game and being only concerned with the kill. If we look more closely at what goes on in practice, it can soon be seen that women play an important role in hunting and trapping smaller animals and in butchering and processing the kills. They often contribute a substantial part of the meat part of a diet in colder climates where plant foods are not as important as in the tropics. Because of their commitment to feeding and looking after children, many women do not range as far from camps as men, although there are cultures where, both before they have children and after they have stopped having children, women do range as far as the men.

How do these general principles apply to Scotland? We suspect that there would have been variations. If people were beginning to modify their environment through fire or pruning

trees to encourage fruiting or the production of long straight branches, they were beginning to invest in resources and would therefore probably have begun to develop ideas of ownership. Of areas where hunter-gatherers were recorded in the recent past, the Scottish environment is most like the north-west coast of America, and here hunter-gatherers were very different from the general picture. Possibly because of the abundance of salmon in their rivers, some of the North American Indians were able to develop a settled society, with elaborate art, warfare, and many of the traits most commonly associated within farmers and more modern societies. Part of the explanation for this may lie in the nature of their exploitation of salmon. They built permanent installations to trap fish as they went up river. These required a considerable amount of work, as did the processing of the seasonal catch, which then had to be stored over the rest of the year. Although using a wild resource, they exploited it in a manner perhaps more akin to farming.

In another aspect, given our northern latitude, it seems reasonable to expect that women would have played a role in hunting, as well as in fishing and plant gathering. We do not know how important hunting was, but given the sites away from the coast, up in the hills, we can estimate that hunting was an important activity. Some big game hunting did occur; we have the bone and antler tools from the middens to show for it. Some of this may have had a social role like much modern hunting – Steve Mithen has shown from a detailed analysis of Danish bone collections that hunting there, where much of the protein would have been met by sea foods, was probably associated with prestige, with people going out of their way to hunt large animals, rather than following the most economically sensible food collecting strategy. We know that sea foods were important to some Mesolithic communities in Scotland, but we should be cautious about assuming that sea foods were important to all of them. It is likely that communities sailing between the islands of the west coast relied far more on the sea than did their cousins on the mainland. Indeed, in terms of avoiding risks, it might be important that different groups did have different bases for their food economies, as it would be less likely for everything to go wrong all at once.

Discovering the Mesolithic Today

The Mesolithic in Scotland is a difficult period to study. Sites are few and far between, poorly preserved and hard to interpret. To make matters still more difficult, the people who left these few remains would have belonged to a society very different from ours, who may have seen their world through very different eyes. They are likely to have seen a world that was much more alive than ours, where every tree or hill may have had a spirit or been associated with past times or mythical stories, or where the soul of a man might inhabit a dog after his death. They would have known few other people, and had few things they called their own. In some ways it is easy to be envious of them, but then it is worth remembering the Scottish winters spent without houses, the dangers of travelling between islands in primitive open boats, and how comfortable modern life has become.

The Mesolithic was a long time ago, but perhaps we can still learn something about our own view of the world by trying to imagine how these people saw Scotland. The last remnants of their nomadic lifestyle may have finally disappeared as the last tinkers disappeared from the country, but people still sometimes try to hark back to this early way of life.

Do not be fooled by ideas of a people living in a hazy dream time at one with nature. Long before the arrival of the hunting rifle, people were the most dangerous and efficient predators in the forests. Within their own abilities they modified their environment for their own needs. Their way of life was a great success: in one form or another hunting and gathering has been the economic and social way of life for nearly all prehistory, and it has survived until the present day in parts of the world where no other system could work. What it could not do was support the levels of population, or social complexities, on which our own civilisation is built.

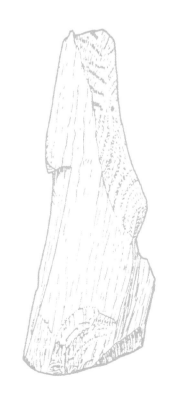

Sites to Visit

As little remains of Mesolithic sites other than flint scatters, overgrown shell middens and buried pits, there is little to see at most site locations. What you can see are the positions of the sites in the landscape, but even with these you must bear in mind that sea levels may have changed, and that land use will have altered completely. Some good places to visit are Gleann Mor on Islay, where the location on a knoll above the glen would have allowed good views of game movements, the Oronsay middens, where, although the island is much bigger nowadays, you can imagine the island life, or Kinloch Farm on Rhum, with its location within the bay. On the mainland Loch Doon in Dumfries and Galloway will provide an indication of an upland location favoured by hunter-gatherers. A drive along the north shore of the Solway Firth will let you see an area with many settlements, while a drive around the base of the cliffs at Oban will let you see the general location of the cave midden sites. The Tweed valley provides another general area where hunter-gatherers once lived, richer than most of the other landscapes.

Island Sites
Map showing location of Mesolithic sites around the Scottish west coast and Inner Hebrides.

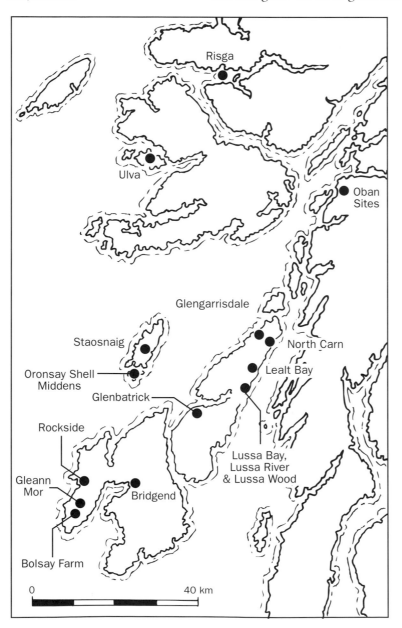

Further Reading

- *The early prehistory of Scotland*, edited by Tony Pollard and Alex Morrison (Edinburgh University Press 1996), contains a set of up-to-date research papers on the Mesolithic.

- *Scotland: Environment and Archaeology, 8000 BC–AD 1000*, edited by Kevin Edwards and Ian Ralston (Wiley 1997), provides sections describing the environment and the Mesolithic.

- *Scotland's First Settlers*, by Caroline Wickham-Jones (Batsford and Historic Scotland 1994) is a general overview of the Mesolithic.

- *Excavations on Oronsay: prehistoric human ecology on a small island*, by Paul Mellars (Edinburgh University Press 1987) provides an account of the principle modern excavation of shell middens.

- *Rhum: Mesolithic and later sites at Kinloch. Excavations 1984-1986* (Society of Antiquaries of Scotland Monograph Series 1990) is Caroline Wickham-Jones's account of her major excavation.

- Peter Woodman published a detailed review in the *Proceedings of the Society of Antiquaries of Scotland for 1989* titled 'Review of the Scottish Mesolithic: a plea for normality'.

- *Farmers, Temples and Tombs*, Gordon Barclay (Canongate 1998), is the next book in The Making Of Scotland series which takes up the story of Scotland's first settlers from around 4000 BC.

Acknowledgements

I would like to thank all those who I worked with on the Mesolithic, and who have provided the inspiration for my thoughts, especially Clive Bonsall, Nyree Finlay, Steve Mithen, Tony Pollard and in particular Caroline Wickham-Jones who commented on an early version of this text and who has helped with the pictures. Alan Barnard, Geraint Coles, Mike Cressey, Ian Ralston and Joe Rock, all of The University of Edinburgh, and Alan Saville of the National Museums of Scotland, all provided assistance with illustrations. The illustrations on p.23 (centre) and p.23 (bottom) are taken from *The Oxford Illustrated Prehistory of Europe*, edited by Barry Cunliffe (Oxford University Press 1994) by permission of Oxford University Press. Harry Bland's questions about how to paint Mesolithic people helped to focus my own ideas. Gordon Barclay not only asked me to write the book but provided encouragement during the process. Thanks are also due to my family, Heather, Amy and Simon, who were forced to read early drafts. The maps were prepared by Sylvia Stevenson and Robert Burns.